Tales from the Crypt
of an American Working Class Hero

More Confessions of a Bipolar Rock and Roller

Rob McCuen

Edited and Designed by Paul J. Hoffman

PathBinder
Publishing LLC
COLUMBUS, INDIANA

First Printing: 2020

.

ISBN 978-1-955088-64-0

PathBinder Publishing
P.O. Box 2611
Columbus, IN 47202

Contents

Forward I (By Rob Friedman)   4
Forward II (By Judith Ann Moriarty)   5

Stories

A Day in the Life of a Sprint Car Rookie   7
Cheap Trick   10
Put 'Em Up, Buster   13
When You Know You've Got it Bad   17
Who The Hell do I Think I am Anyway?   20

Lyrics

Another Drive By Shooting   23
Another Nail in My Cross   24
Brains in a Jar   25
Crack, The   26
Cuz Rock is Dead   27
Daddy Only Dreamin'   28
Empty Handed Again   29
For My Beloved Son, Sean Robert   30
For Sheilia   31
Hole to Crawl in, A   32
I Love Myself   33
I'm A.J. Foyt   34
John Lennon   35
Life Imitates Art   36
Life on the Rocks   37
Money Can't Buy Me   38
Monkey Sees, The   39
(O Boy) Are You a Man or a Mouse?   40
Poison Pen, The   41
Torch Song   42
When I'm Depressed   43
White Trash   44
World is Full of Clowns, The   45

About the Author   46

Forward I

"Paradox" is an overused word, but it might be the only word that approximates the writer of these stories.

I only knew Rob McCuen as a dark figure that drew grunts and rolled eyes among the musicians that I knew in the Milwaukee alternate music scene. I had no idea that he wrote anything but lyrics to some pop/garage/punk songs I'd heard and liked. Or that he published hundreds of articles in international racing magazines (and drove those same cars).

I knew he'd fronted some popular bands and was the drummer for Plasticland – arguably the best psychedelic band of the '80s in the world. No small claim.

Then I lucked into playing with him in my basement for the last three years. Loud and driving and determined to form a duet that would play the local dives. I was unwilling, but I got to taste not only the drummer but also the quiet, deeply caring guy that is hidden behind the bravado.

He is funny as fuck and will suffer no bullshit, though he will make up stories like the one where the tiny dog he babysits for was shot out of the sky, and into the clutches of an eagle as he watched. I bought it. He's a cutthroat writer and liver of life.

So I'll shut up and let the stories take you. Enjoy.

—Robert Friedman

Forward II

We collided in the lobby of the legendary Shorecrest Hotel. It was the late '90s. Rob was trying to untangle his Iowa roots and I was assembling my Iowa roots.

I thought his name was Rod McCune.

"No," he smirked, "the name's Rob McCuen, and I'm a writer. Here, read this short story," he fairly commanded.

I took it to my apartment on floor four and gave it a once over and decided McCuen's use of the F-word was as a sign that he couldn't think of other adjectives to save his neck. We met again later in the lobby, and I told him his story was too vulgar.

I don't recall him speaking to me for a year. He was a pretty boy from another era, a rock and roll drummer, singer, songwriter, now author on the lam from Iowa. I know the feeling, although my Iowaay was big band and all-night movies in my boyfriend's Buick Roadmaster when I was just 15.

Rob McCuen is no longer a pretty boy (um ... yes I am. haha — Rob) and the thin, onion skin ego has peeled away over the decades. Somewhere underneath all the cocksure bravado, Rob has softened some. But make no mistake, the boy has an edge that crackles like lightning. The real Rob has emerged, or should I say survived.

There was a time when he called me "Battle Axe," but over our hard-earned friendship, he's shortened it to simply "Axe," a term of endearment, I suppose.

McCuen, after at least two suicide attempts, seems to at long last be ready to become his own best friend.

— Judith Ann Moriarty, a longtime freelance writer and artist
and former owner of *Art Muscle* magazine

STORIES

A Day in the Life of a Sprint Car Rookie

It began with an innocent question, and it haunts my dear old dad to this very day, may he rest in eternal peace.

"Robbie, how would you like me to take you to the sprint car races tonight at the Henry County Fair?"

I was six years old and didn't know a sprint car from a monkey's ass, but the tingling in my spine told me volumes about what I might be in for. The undeniable and overwhelming rush of first love. Think Vickee Lewis in sixth grade, only heavier than even that.

I can still recall my response in vivid detail. "What's a sprint car, Daddy? Are they faster than Mississippi Valley Speedway Club jalopies?"

Sprint cars are like small Indy cars with just as much horsepower," said my daddy by way of explanation. "And yes, they're *a lot* faster than those old crates."

That's all it took.

I was in a frenzy. I might have been a snot-nosed punk, but I was already a seasoned racing freak. Every winter, we tore our tricked-out Stingray bicycles down to the bare frame because that's what they did in Gasoline Alley over Indianapolis way. I'd been watching jalopies churn the sacred dirt for three years already and I knew my onions. I'd also seen go-karts, micro-midgets and 3/4 midgets on a high-banked, one-tenth mile oval on the outskirts of Mount Pleasant, Iowa. We were an unabashed racing town back in '59, and that suited me just fine, thank you very much.

Sure, I liked Mickey Mantle, but I was completely obsessed with Jimmy Bryan, Don "Gramps" Branson, Jim Rathman, Roger Ward and some punk kid from Houston who called himself A.J. Foyt. In the primitive terrain where a young boy operates, I fell in love with racing from my first green flag on. But the *fever* was about to turn lethal.

"There's a sprint car on the trailer over at Eland's Sinclair, driven by Harold Leep, from down Wichita way. He won the Hawkeye Futurity yesterday in Des Moines. Would you like to see it?"

We rounded the tree-lined S-curve on U.S. Highway 218, and lo and behold, there she sat, scarlet and chrome glistening in the mid-afternoon sun, a silver No. 52 adorning her pointed, graceful tail tank. She was shaped like a backward bullet, her leather cockpit barely large enough to accommodate a man. She looked sleek and fast and menacing sitting there on the trailer all by her lonesome, her knobby tires sticking out like swollen fingers.

Everything changed from that moment forward. All I would ever need in life was right there before my eyes in the form of this purebred and sinister mass of motor, fiberglass, and chrome moly metal. This was what social scientists refer to as a "moment of clarity," and in this instant, I knew two things: I had to see this gorgeous, macho machine turned loose on the holy half-mile, and someday, no matter the cost, I was gonna drive a sprint car. I was gonna be the best who ever lived.

Forty years later, I got my wish.

First and foremost, Randy Sippel is a race car driver. Not a renowned one, but a sprint car driver nonetheless. His school in Elkhart Lake, Wisconsin, will sell you a dream and the thrill of a lifetime at a fraction of the cost of fielding your own sprinter. Together, Sippel and four-time Interstate Racing Association's Gib Wiser combined for fifty years in the business of going fast. After a brief lesson in the intricacies of chassis set-up and an instructional chapter on how to belt in and bail out in case of fire, it was at long last time to get it on.

We were a curious lot, from all walks of life, eighteen men and four women ranging in age from 22 to 49. Each participant is given three seven-lap dashes, alone on the track to my dismay. But nonetheless, this was a defining moment for me, a 46-year-old writer, rocker and painting contractor.

I decided to take two sessions in the micro before I strapped on the 360-cubic-inch sprinter to get myself acclimated. I gave my belts a final tug, eased off the clutch … and I was off, not a trace of nerves.

I would love to be able to say that I headed straight for the cushion, but that would be a bold-faced lie. I was no slug, but track records were for dreamers. It took me two laps to put the pedal all the way to the bellypan, and my corner entries were too low to build any real speed. Momentum is what it's all about.

I felt the car leaning way over on the right rear, and I tried to ignore the sensation that it was going to turn over on me. The track surface was hard and slick, and there was little or no cushion to lean on. And I knew I was fighting the race car as I tried in vain to find my comfort zone.

I was calm as a kitten, and as I began to hold the hammer down a little longer in the chutes, to hit my marks as it were, the car got instantly easier to drive. The wing began to work as my corner speeds went up, and my confidence soared.

Randy was frantically waving a black flag at me in a futile attempt to coerce me into slowing down. I wasn't having any of that and I pushed it even harder. Caution was for wimps, and as wild man Carmen Manzardo looked on, I was becoming a race car driver. The only thing missing was traffic to dice with. I had fleeting images of my father, Jan Opperman, and that punk, Foyt.

It never occurred to me how much it would cost me if I wadded up one of Sippel's hotrods. I wondered if I was as fast as I felt, but I was pretty sure I wasn't. Everybody, including the great Doug Wolfgang, told me that keeping a race car off the fence is a lot harder than it looks from the stands. I never doubted it, so I stood on it even harder.

"Wait until I strap into the full blown sprinter. I'll blow their minds," I said aloud.

Reality at speed takes on a surreal quality that would be easy to get hooked on. My seven laps were over in a flash of dust and brimstone. I'd been lost in a feverish time warp.

The second session was more of the same, only faster and better. The track had been watered some, so I had to feather the throttle a bit more. But it was already starting to seem familiar. I ran a higher line and got completely out of shape on the now built-up, but albeit modest, "cushion." The car seemed to be bogging down in the apexes of the corners, and when I pulled in, now a fourteen-year "veteran," Sippel and Wiser couldn't contain their glee. I was a fucking prodigy.

"You're not the kind of guy who is willing to work up to speed, are ya, kid?" Wiser asked.

But screw micros, they were mere toys in my hands, and I longed to jump in the 360. I had perhaps been a little edgy in the mini, but I felt no trace of fear until I buckled into the sprinter.

I switched on the fuel line, jammed it into gear, felt the push truck brush my rear bumper, and I was off. Five hundred horsepower rumbled to life.

Oh boy, it was show time.

I wasted no time punching the throttle all the way to the mat on the back chute. I could tell the race car wasn't geared for maximum torque to keep idiots like me off the rails, but this was sheer bliss!

There were no more random thoughts of Opperman, or even my father. I was busy in the cramped cockpit with a mile-wide smile. This was living, baby. I was a race car driver, big and fast and brave ...

Cheap Trick

It was only 1976, and Cheap Trick were still assaulting every toilet, dive, and joint they could find. The world wasn't onto them yet, but two bars into "ELO Kiddies," and my world had changed forever. Yep, right up there with seeing the Beatles on Ed Sullivan.

The world wasn't onto them yet, but I was, and I wasn't alone. My friends and I were sporting ties for everyday use just like Robin Zander. The message was loud and clear: a new Fab Four were upon us in the form of Rick, Robin, Tom, and Bun, and they were gonna save rock and roll.

Suddenly a whole new set of rules kicked in. The lads were from Rockford, Illinois, for Christ sakes, and that made anything possible. Maybe you could launch a career without moving to La La land after all.

Cheap Trick, already too well traveled to be considered Midwestern hayseeds, were throwing themselves into the rock and roll blender right before my eyes. Clearly, a band this over the top could be based anywhere they chose.

No scene, no problem. "We'll create the scene." They tried Europe in an earlier incarnation, billed as Sick Man of Europe, but their already finely honed instincts told them that the Midwest could be converted into their own world.

Almost overnight, the cool-o-meter in the heartland got a muchneeded karate chop to the throat. They'd blow into town in a white limousine, blow yer fucking mind, and be gone before you knew what hit ya. It was high voltage rape and pillage, and Cheap Trick were on the warpath, makeup intact.

The first record wasn't even out yet. But if you saw 'em then, there could be no denying their impact. The muthafuckers were gonna be huge … and soon. The band knew it, too, and it was a beautiful thing to witness up close and personal. They were still *our* band, but we knew it wouldn't last, and we were gonna have to share them with the rest of the universe.

Even though they were still pounding the bar circuit from Bismark to Beloit, they were already stars, waving to fans in imaginary arenas in the non-existent balcony. Nielsen had a vision, and there would be no stopping it. Rick was a shrewd and savvy businessman and was, along with personal manager and resident sleazeball Ken Adamany, determined to hold out for a long-term recording contract.

The bidding wars soon began. Timing in the hyperfickle world of pop music was everything, and the Tricksters were in this shit for the long haul. Critics, street urchins, intellectuals and Bohemians alike were fawning over the bastard child that was punk RAWK, and while the Trick warmly embraced the punk ethos, they were also wary of its limitations.

Their collective vision, which unapologetically included having massive hit records and radio airplay, was far too vast for platitudes, musical or otherwise. For starters, Cheap Trick had a unique way of processing their diverse influences and included wearing their love for the Beatles on their sleeves. But their resource pool also included heavy doses of Kinks, The Who, The Family, T. Rex, Raspberries, Dylan, and even the Velvet Underground.

Somehow, it all made sense, and by the time all that ran through the power pop blender, they still sounded like Cheap Trick. They were lean, mean, hungry, and fierce, and they were young and brash. Even Nielsen, the elder statesman and chief visionary was only 31.

Robin, the thin man with a thousand voices may have looked like a frail teen idol, but when he kicked up his heels and delivered the knockout punch, no one could touch him. Zander was only 22. Their sound was one of unmatched power, majesty, swagger, wit, charm, and fury. They were equal parts raw, polished, riveting, violent, immediate, intense, tragic, hilarious, hauntingly beautiful, and hysterical. They were also in your face and louder than a squadron of jet fighter planes.

The songcraft was a foregone conclusion, rich in melody and lyrically sublime, playful, rife with double and triple entendres. It was smart pop for smart people, and even if you were a late-to-the-party village idiot, the lads could slap you senseless with the sheer force of their Cap'n Crunch power chords. It was all in a night's work for our lads.

And they didn't discriminate. Glue sniffers, hopheads, suburb buzzards, trannies, scenesters, gas-huffers, power poppers, New Wavers, art fags, burnouts, punks, rubes, city slickers, and divas alike were along for the ride. By the time Trick bade you "auf wiedersein," they owned ya for a lifetime, and they knew it.

They were cocky to the point of arrogance at times, as any great band must be, but were refreshingly accessible when their workday was done. Nielsen could be seen in arenas accepting back slaps and shots at the bar when they were a mere opening act. Whether on stage or off, you could never be sure if they were mocking or celebrating rock stardom, but they made it seem more fun than anyone working the boards at the time.

Cheap Trick's visual presentation was stunning, wildly at odds with conventional presentations, like a page torn from the theater of the absurd. Somehow, the image was perfect and all their own. Still, you couldn't quite shake the notion that the whole act was on colossal puton, and the joke was on us.

They may have looked like they were having a giant lark at our expense, but they had a genuine affection for their fans. Each in his own way was a stellar showman. Bun's celebrated if studied geekdom, Rick's hyper Donald Sutherland meets Huntz Hall, Robin's brain boiling good looks and Tom's svelte charm.

Fast forward to 2003. Cheap Trick, stardom firmly intact, released the stellar "Special One," and though widely panned, was a fan's wet dream. Their place in history perches precariously between full-blown stardom and the ultimate cult group. So granted, maybe they don't deliver the knockout blow every night like the Trick in their prime, but there isn't enough Viagra on the planet for the Rolling Stones to go face to with the Trick, even on the rare off night. And there are no alt bands that can hold up to Cheap Trick, either. They are warriors, and even age can't dim their decided brilliance.

Critics have been trying to write them off for twenty-odd years, and that, my friends, is a huge mistake. Everyone thought they were doomed when Tom flew the coop in 1980 to field a lame Missing Persons knockoff. But Petersson came to his senses and returned to the fold just in time for a commercial resurgence when they released "The Flame," which the band hated. I once asked Tom at a cream show in Hartford, Wisconsin, who wrote this vapid ballad, and Tom sneered, "I dunno, some English fag." Hilarious.

The band also transcended a bitter split with longtime manager Ken Adamany and left Epic under the worst of terms. Still, Cheap Trick soldiered on, seemingly unfazed by the smaller rooms they were once again relegated to playing in. They'd made a record with George Martin and played the planet's most prestigious venues and headlined all over the world.

A lesser band might have called it a career, but not our four lads. They just keep on doing what they've always done, rocking you until your body parts start melting. Fuck being on top of the world, they'd already been there. They can do whatever they want cuz they're the fabulous Cheap Trick.

Any questions???

Put 'Em Up, Buster

Me and John Fitzgerald hated each other 's guts from kindergarten on. We didn't need a reason. And therein lies the fucking beauty. That's part of the charm of being a kid. Relationships have no pretense. Problem solving couldn't have been more simple — ya put up your fucking dukes or you shut the fuck up.

By the time we hit the fourth grade running, it was full-scale war. Even insults were beneath the both of us. When it was go-go time, there were never any preliminaries. A well-placed jab and uppercut was worth a thousand idle words. It's funny though, for a couple of guys who hated each other so much, our communication skills were finely honed. All it took was a well-placed look, and it was always enough to say it all.

"Wanna try me, punk?"

"So fuck you and let's rumble."

Permanent disfigurement was the eternal goal, and I still sleep more soundly even these days knowing that Fitzgerald still thinks of me every time he yawns from one of my expertly implemented right hooks, his nose bent over like a palm tree in a fucking hurricane.

It serves the dirty bastard right, doncha think? Evertime I fucking yawn, my jaw still cracks, snaps, and pops. The bastard hit me so hard it felt like I had been stunned with a Louisville Slugger.

We were a study in contrasts. For starters, the cocksucker outweighed me by sixty pounds. I was hung up on the aesthetics of fist fighting, bobbing, weaving. Ducking, and jabbing, always leading with my left to set him up for the right uppercut.

Sure, I wanted to flat kill him, but I wanted to look like a young Cassius Clay in the process. I was a boxer, and Fitzy was a killing machine. But seeing him seethe with green envy over by the pinball machine with his slime slug buddies while I mauled poor Dee Dee "Hot Pants" Rodd almost made my broken right wing all worthwhile. Fitzy had twisted me into a pretzel and I took a savage beating over Labor Day weekend. John was a bulldozer, advancing, always advancing. Sometimes, he'd get wreckless and leave himself open to the best punch in my arsenal: my famous right uppercut.

Except for one lousy detail. Even with the tits of my adolescent dreams heaving in and out of my blurred vision, I came to the harshest fact of my life.

This was the third time in a row that he'd nearly peeled me from my bones, and each time he was hurting me more and taking less time to do me in.

But I never quit. I'd had 85 bouts and I only lost five counting the two I lost to Stanley "Gramps" Ford cuz I called him a blow boy. Guess what? Five bucks and you were all his, the bloated toad.

I never indulged, but some of my friends did. How was I gonna tell my dad that I'd lost another fight, and this time I got my goddamn arm busted almost clean in two?

"Face the fucking music, buddy boy. Fitzy is badder than you," said a tiny but irrepressible voice inside of my ringing head. And I knew this to be true, hard as it was to fess up.

My mind drifted back to happier times, like the time I made the beaten bloody bastard lick my boots while the whole fifth grade cheered me on. Where was Dee Dee Rodd when I needed her most? I thought about my two death blows — TKOs — but that was clear back in fourth grade. This was high school for Christ sakes, and I couldn't bear the thought of being punch drunk and washed up at eleven. I vowed Fitzy was gonna pay for his dastardly deeds. It was time to get serious.

I wasted no time plotting my comeback. I trained like a Marine with something extra special to prove, if only to myself. I pumped iron, I skipped rope, I relentlessly pounded on the speed bag and ran three miles a day. I quit cigarettes cold and protein builders became my drink of choice. I was a man on a mission.

It didn't help that my wing was still wounded and I couldn't play freshman football. And wouldn't you know it, Fitzgerald was a wreckless bowling ball, a star linebacker. Fitzy made first-team all-conference while I smoldered sullenly in the stands with all the other wannabe fux.

It was late November before I finally had the nerve to cut the cast off. In January, I tried him again while we were in gym class playing killer dodgeball. I drilled him in the honker at point blank range, and blood squirted from his face like I'd attacked him with a hatchet.

"You'll die for this, 'Bone,'" sputtered Fitzgerald through clenched teeth.

Uh oh, what have I done, now? He only calls me "Bone" when he's super atomic pissed off. Fitzy lunged at me like a wounded police dog, those killer brown eyes of his glazed over with rage.

I saw my opening and took it. I clubbed him with a quick jab to his midsection, and when he dropped his guard to cover up, I circled left and straightened him up with my famous left jab to the mouth. The uppercut of a lifetime dropped him like a clubbed seal, put his punk ass to sleep.

"Pleasant dreams, four-eyes," I crowed while planting my foot triumphantly on his chest.

My victory celebration was cut short by Coach Skowronski, who was as famous for his fierce temper as he was for treating physical ed like Marine boot camp.

"That was a cheap shot, McCuen. Now get your scrawny ass to the principal's office. Now," he bellowed, his Pillsbury Doughboy face only inches from mine.

Now old man Stafford had been head honcho for damn near thirty years, and the only real joy left in his fading life came from enforcing his ironclad fucking rules with punks like me. He considered fistfights to be right up there with first-degree murder. Stafford sentenced me to a three-day suspension, which felt more like a vacation than punishment. I hated school, and I sucked at it, a lifelong C student.

Besides, I figured the old man was doing me a favor. I wanted to stay as far away from Fitzy as possible as I knew he was already plotting his revenge. He wasn't the kind of guy who was gonna take a public humiliation such as this without quickly settling the score. And yeah, throwing a basketball at his face *was* a cheap shot, but so fucking what? This was John Fitzgerald, and I didn't see how a little ole thing like ethics had a goddamn thing to do with it. I should've killed him while I had the chance.

"McCuen's gonna spend the rest of his sorry ass life in a wheelchair, " he was heard muttering within earshot of my friend, Scotty the spy. So I did what any self-respecting cheap shot artist would do. I dodged him, hoping I could sidestep him until I was old enough to grow up and move to Siberia, where he could never find me. A wheelchair didn't mesh with my master plan to become an all-star defensive back and world class drummer.

I began to entertain the notion of an early retirement from brawling. That was the trouble with most fighters anyway. They hung around too long, and I really wasn't sure how many more serious head shots I could withstand without being turned into a vegetable. Some days, my brain felt like instant pudding.

It was tough giving ole Fitzy the slip in a town as small as Mount Pleasant, especially since I had to be careful to appear as though I was not doing just that very thing. I might have turned chicken, but I still had my gunslinger reputation to preserve. I'd never backed down from anybody. Besides, I'd started smoking dope, and I dunno, it's hard to explain, but somehow I didn't feel much like fighting anymore. Now I'm not for a minute implying that I'd turned into some mantra chanting, bongo beating, peacenik hippie or anything, but the kind bud was taking me to new corners of my brain.

Of course, my arch nemesis had undergone no such transformation. He just wanted to tear my head loose from my neck. I managed to steer clear of him for damn near three months. My luck finally ran out one Friday night at Fatty's Pizza Palace. Fitzy, like a wild pig, had just made seventeen solo tackles against Fairfield, and he was all pumped up. Dee Dee Rodd was even there.

Fitzy was drunk, and he had that spooky fucking look in his eyes again and was all pumped up from post-football adrenaline. He charged me like a wounded rooster and pinned me against the jukebox in an effort to shove my face through the glass.

"Play 'Spirit in the Sky, ' motherfucker, " he said cuz he knew I hated that song like no other. Lucky for me, I had a friend in Fatty's, and he grabbed Fitzy by the throat and threatened to throw his punk ass in a pizza oven.

I'd dodged another bullet, but I knew this wasn't over … not by a long shot.

Three days later, I was motoring west on Clay Street in the '67 Mustang convertible that I'd filched from my mother while she was at bridge club. I reached over to crank the treble past the threshold of pain as Smokey Robinson's "Going to a Go-Go" threatened to reduce the cheap-ass factory speakers to dust.

By the time I saw her, it was too fucking late. I stomped and stabbed at the brake pedal, and the Mustang screeched to a halt. Fearing the worst, I jumped out, and there it was, a puppy, yelping and writhing on the blood-stained pavement, mortally wounded, her tiny chest heaving in and out convulsively. I huddled over her, praying silently between fits of tears, helpless and heartbroken.

I heard footsteps coming toward me, but I was too freaked out to look up.

"What happened? How could you?" said the voice.

I froze. That fucking voice. It couldn't be ... but it was.

It was Fitzy, and he just stood there crying and shaking his massive mastodon head from side to side.

"That's Taffy you hit, my little sister Margaret's dog," he said without a trace of menace. He sounded lost and he looked that way, too.

"I'm sorry, John, I never even saw her," I stammered.

"Please don't die," Fitzy stammered over and over again. "Please don't die."

Taffy was going into shock and I got up to get a blanket out of the trunk.

"Never mind, man. Taffy's gone," Fitzy said in his weakest voice yet. We stood there dazed and lost, no one speaking. Finally, ole' Fitzy fished a crumpled pack of Parliments out of his Army jacket, which was emblazoned with Black Sabbath patches. I nodded and tried to speak, but Fitzy stopped me cold in my tracks.

"You don't have to explain. I know you didn't mean to do it, man."

We smoked in silence, alone with our thoughts, but still keenly aware of each other. Fitzy cleared his voice to speak, and I looked deep into his tear-soaked eyes. The meanest eyes I'd ever seen didn't look so mean anymore.

We reached for each other with the same suddenness that had made our fights the stuff of legend. No preliminaries, No bullshit. No pretension. We just stood there embracing, crying without shame. Two fourteen-year-old boys with all our macho stripped clean away.

Me and Fitzy never became friends, but we never had another brawl. Only last year, I went to his funeral. Rest in Peace, old rival. God speed.

When You Know You've Got It Bad

He had it for her bad. I mean super atomic bad, like full blown out of his skull. Russel was seventeen, too young and too driven by his raging hormones to recognize it for what it really was. But she was the setting sun to him, the air that he breathed, and a life without her was well, not even worth living in.

A few years later, as a team of white coats methodically picked away at Russel's brain, they hung some clinical names on him, and that was that. They concluded that Russel was suffering from delusions and acute obsession.

Russel told them to go fuck themselves. The only thing he was suffering from was *love* of the purest order. The doctors politely smiled their collective condescending smiles.

Russel was still a virgin, the only one he knew, and he aimed to keep it that way until she was all his.

"Why doncha just score yourself a whore?" his best friend, Donny, would always say whenever the tender subject came up.

But Russel didn't want a whore, he wanted only *her*. He didn't really expect anyone to understand that she was his destiny, a deal he'd made with the Lord. He never cheapened it by talking about it; he just knew deep inside his mind that she was his to have and to hold, forever. He was being guided by a higher force, and all he had to do was listen to the voices bouncing around in his head.

He'd been in love with her for three glorious years, tortuous, agonizing beautiful beyond description years. He was only fourteen when he's seen her on *The Tonight Show*. Russel went out and got all her records and bought three copies of every magazine she ever graced the cover of.

It was then that he heard her sing country. He quit school the next day. The voices got ever louder and told him to hitchhike to California. She would be there waiting for him.

"Sing to her," said the voices, and she will be forever yours.

Russel bought himself a beat-up 12-string Harmony guitar and borrowed a pup tent from his Uncle Eugene. He still had enough dough left over to get to Lincoln, Nebraska, on the Greyhound.

"Your blind love and faith will see you through," said the ever louder voices.

The very next morning, he wedged his huge frame into a corner seat and set off for Hollywood. By four in the afternoon he was in Lincoln, six bucks from vagrancy. Russel treated himself to a nasty cheeseburger and the worst coffee he had ever tasted. Sixty-five cents for a tip, and he was chump change away from being flat broke. He tried to summon the voices but they had fallen eerily silent.

Still and all, he felt strangely calm, jitters and all. He lumbered past a row of tired old shops that couldn't disguise the despair hidden inside. A shoe repair shop, a bakery that reeked of yeast and a men's clothing shop that boasted, "where the well-dressed man gets that way." Abandoned buildings stood forlorn, forgotten as orphans.

Urban decay was eating up the small towns, too. He couldn't explain it, but Russel felt strangely reassured. Who cared why? His pace quickened, his steel wool hair oblivious to the angry autumn wind. Lincoln was his town now, a mere link to his destiny.

He sang his heart out in front of the Majestic, a beat-up but still thriving B-movie theater and made himself twenty bucks and change. He played until he broke two strings and left a few dozen admirers there on the cracked sidewalk and cigarette-tainted street, clamoring for a reprieve from their workday, dreary, despair riddled lives.

"C'mon boy, play some more," they begged.

But Russel barely heard them. He was exhausted, and his soul felt frayed, worn out, like the shops that stood before him. He wandered into a filthy alley and found a place to sleep under some rickety, rotted wooden stairs, a trash bag for a pillow.

A cold drizzle served as his morning wakeup call, the closest to a shower he'd had in three days. Even aching muscles and damp clothes failed to dampen his spirit. In a mere three days, with any luck, *she* would be all his.

As Russel stood on an entrance ramp to Interstate 80, he couldn't help but contemplate the highway's illustrious history, America's first super slab, which was completed in 1975, spanned almost 3,000 miles from New York City all the way to San Francisco. Now she was but an artery in a complex web of four-laners that would forever alter the very infrastructure of the "land of the free." Small towns would be rendered mere ghosts of their former selves, dropped from thriving communities to phantoms, dropped from relevance like forgotten fads. Roadhouse bars, cheap hotels, gas stations and clip joints alike would be erased from amerikkka's collective consciousness with the stoke of a planing commisioner's pen.

The big-money boys licked their chops and moved right in, sensing the death of another town. A Howard Johnson every fifty miles. Fill those big gas guzzlers with Sinclair, for Christ sakes. Feed those road weary travelers fast food until they puke bile. Stick the knife in and twist it twice for good measure, goddamn it. Fuck the Amerikkkan dream. We smell money!

Teddy's Garage and Towing couldn't hold out and hang on forever. "We represent British Petroleum and we are prepared to offer you a handsome profit for your deed, fuck you very much."

Old Teddy might kick and scream all he wanted about his granddaddy starting up the biz from nothing. Let's just wait and see how far family loyalty goes when they reach for the corporate checkbook.

Russel had seen this shit firsthand. His very own daddy had owned a forty-unit motel on the outskirts of Kenosha for almost twenty-five years. It had flourished for the better part of two decades, and then, practically overnight, the vultures swept in and wiped him out. Folks wanted convenience and familiarity, or so they were told.

Russel's daddy hadn't been so lucky, too far from an exit ramp. Nobody was buying into old world charm and breakfast in bed anymore. Russel's daddy lived out his final frail days working the front desk of a Best Western in Lexington, Kentucky. Yet here Russel was, just another chump forsaking the blood and guts of backwater Amerikkka for the sheer convenience of another four lanes of super slab.

To be continued...

Who the Hell Do I Think I am Anyway?

I had always thought that today was my birthday. Well HAPPY FUCKING BIRTHDAY, sucker! All of these goddamned years, I thought, for all my shortcomings, I at the very least had a firm grip on my identity. I didn't always like what I saw, but I knew who I was.

But I guess not. Never mind that I had to rifle through my parents' bottom drawer to learn the God awful truth. And hell yeah, I helped myself to $60 and chump change in the process, but so fucking what? They got off cheap. A lesser man would've burned their house to the fucking ground with them in it. But revenge can wait a while. I wanna watch 'em squirm, the lowdown maggots.

Why didn't they just hack up the truth? I could've handled it.

"We're sorry, but we're not your real parents. You're adopted." Simple.

How could they have perpetuated such a colossal stack of lies? How could they have covered their tracks so completely?

But in the end, they underestimated me. Maybe they thought I had too much character to go snooping around in their desk. But now they know different, and so do I. I'm not who I thought I was, not by a long shot.

Old Ted and Betty, those pillar of the community, God-fearing folks cut straight from a Norman Rockwell painting lied to me about everything: where I was born, my lineage, even my fucking age. I was by far the smallest kid in school. I wasn't a boy; I was a goddamn rhesus monkey, a laboratory experiment gone horribly awry.

I grew up being told I was born on December 1, 1957, the only son of a spare-the-rod-and-spoil-the-child banking executive and a milk-andcookies housewife cut clean from the cloth of Jackie Kennedy. But alas, as I learned a mere six weeks ago, lies, all lies.

I now know that my father was a two-bit pool hustler, a hard-drinkin', hell raisin' preacher 's son from Tuscaloosa, Alabama, who worked as a lowly sharecropper when his gambling got the best of him, which was nearly always. My mama was a longshoreman from Middletown, Pennsylvania. Their names are Milton and Babs Silverstein, and I think they're still alive, but not for long if I have a say in it. Apparently, my old man also dabbled in professional wrestling in the late '50s under the name "Chester the Molester" and my mama was a world-class card shark and hypnotist. I've got four brothers and seven sisters, but for some unforeseen reason, I was the only one they ditched on.

My adoptive parents found me in the back of a rusty station wagon in downtown Miami, where they were honeymooning in late '59. This is where my cruel odyssey truly begins. It seems they wanted a child, but weren't real keen on the notion of the commitment of child rearing. So they concocted an elaborate scheme whereby everything concerning me was projected ahead ten years. This way, they figured they could coerce me into growing up and moving away by the time I was ten years old. Learned wannabe "scholars" that they were, they were fascinated with the ramifications of studying the social side effects of assimilating a child who thought he was much older than he actually was.

Imagine what it's been like for poor little old me. I graduated high school when I was only eight years old. I, of course, was bamboozled into thinking I was eighteen.

"Mother," I'd squeak in my little prepubescent voice, "why am I so small? The kids are always making fun of me."

"Perhaps it's poor nutrition, dear. Have a glass of milk and a banana." And I fucking bought it. My classmates called me "sawed off" and "mayor of the munchkins." Then, adding insult to injury, my school made me its school mascot. I had to don a tiny panther cub suit and they'd wheel me into the gymnasium in a gaudily painted circus wagon. As a result, I became a statewide phenom, a legend in my own time warp world. I was regarded as a cute little freak of nature, and I began to receive correspondence from carnivals requesting my services as a sideshow freak attraction.

My parents, ever the opportunists, assumed the role of my agent and force-fed me a five-year contract with Burn's and Bosley's Million Dollar Shrine Circus, working the state fair circuit. It was here that I got my first taste of the show biz life. I was paid $35 a week and was given all the cabbage I could eat.

After I fell in love with Wanda the Pretzel Girl (imagine the possibilities), it really wasn't such a bad life. We lived together in a 6x10 wagon alongside "Rubber Boy." The wagon was well stocked with freshly mown hay and a couple of horse blankets. I was billed as "Timmy, the World's Tiniest Teenager." I had a juggling act, and me and Wanda were hit attractions. We did nine shows a day, 250 dates a year. We wintered in Florida and were given our very own barn with water from a pig sewer to sustain us.

These were the happiest days of my life!

I had a blossoming career in show business and the girl of my dreams. But then, the bottom fell out of my star time life forever. I began to grow. My once mighty following dwindled to a trickle almost overnight, and near the end of my contract renewal, old man Bosley voided my contract and Wanda dumped me for "Frog Boy." Frog Boy paid no dues; he had risen through the freak show ranks practically overnight, and just like that was all the rage.

I was washed up, driven out of the only life I had known. So I was always stuck at the bottom of the bill, a lowly opening act. I tried the midget wrestling circuit for a time, but I wasn't a real midget.

I didn't know what else to do, so I started robbing gas stations and churches. This proved to be a poor career choice for a ten-year-old kid, even if I did think I was twenty. Nobody took me seriously as a gun totin' stick-up man, and I was soon caught and sent straight to jail. My ever thoughtful parents blamed me for costing them a piece of the TiltA-Whirl action and had me committed to an insane asylum in Hibbing, Minnnesota.

It was there that I learned to play drums from a janitor who used to be in Dion and the Belmonts, I think it was. Finally, after four years in a rubber room and no toilet, they let me out and I joined Plasticland, a psychedelic pop group of foppish dandies with silly haircuts and pointy boots.

Now, here we are fifteen long, hard years later, and I'm still here, longing for the carnival life. My parents are imposters, I'm Jewish, not Irish. And Wanda, the only dame I ever loved, ran off to the Dells with that creepy scaly amphibian "Frog Boy" where they are star attractions with their mutant offspring at Reptile Gardens.

But one good thing came from all of this. My soon to be murdered exparents' cruel scam-o-rama just bought me ten years of time. And that, my friends, is a beautiful thing. I'll turn 56 in July. That's my story so SHUT THE FUK UP!

LYRICS

Another Drive By Shooting

The screaming siren lullaby lulls my family to sleep
even more real than television when blood spills on the streets
i told you before i can't lose i already lost
i just stood by helpless and watched my daddy get shot.

x marks the spot where the innocent stand
he gotta heart full of hate and your head in his hands
you're a blast away from meeting your god
ya better stand back jack he's just doing his job.

Drive by gonna kill ya dead
drive by gonna waste ya
punk's already made his bed
buckets full of blood gonna spill
ya know he lives to kill
another drive by
another drive by shooting.

walking wounded zombies and chalk line ghosts
at the corner of broken dreams boulevard and the lane of no hope
urban guerilla warfare it's a bloodbath carcass store
and nobody fights with their fists anymore.

gang banger assassins will kill ya for sport
we all gonna wind up in the coroner 's report
i told ya before i can't lose i already lost
he know ya got nothin' still he craves whatcha got.

drive by gonna kill ya dead
punk's already made his bed
buckets full of blood gonna spill
they just live to kill
another drive by another drive by shooting...

Another Nail in My Cross

ya burst my bubble baybee what the hell?
i popped your birthday balloons
i sense trouble every single time when it enters my room...

today is your birthday baybee
i'm a prince i didn't forget
you know i'm the king of sabotage
and you're just another nail in my cross...

two days to pick the pieces up
baybee did ya bring your broom?
i see trouble coming down the line
when ya sing that tune.
i thought i knew ya now you're somebody else
they sent ya off to charm school baybee they made into somebody else. another
nail in my cross
another nail in my cross
another day at the cross
another nail in my cross...

finding only thorns in my bed of roses
finding only blood on my holy cross
i grow poison from the seeds i've sewn
now you're just another nail in my cross...

i can only smell trouble they say it comes in threes
planting the seed of the green grass of home.
it only comes up weeds.
you burst my bubble so i popped your birthday balloons
just another nail on my cross..

two days to pick the pieces up baybee did ya bring your broom?
i can sense trouble coming the way you sweep into a room.
you lost your innocence (and me)? i just got lost
and to think you were my savior bayybee
now you're just another nail in my cross!

another nail on my cross...

Brains in a Jar

for the love of danger for the thirst of intrigue
even brains in a jar get hungry with need
for the lust of a stranger for remote control greed even brains in
a jar sometimes they gotta come clean.

will ya track my shadow thru the blood-stained snow? the tick of
a time bomb 'til they swallow you whole quit twisting the heads
off my gi joe
even brains in a jar need somewhere to go.

creep show cretins get so outta line
my heart is beating beating beating in 4/4 time
two kindred spirits our two worlds collide
even brains in a jar are jeckyls and hydes.

even brains in a jar can blow their minds
is that my brain swimming in formaldehyde...

The Crack

well there are cracks in my character and many cracks in my walls
but the jokes i been crackin' ain't so funny at all.
well there are cracks in the sidewalk and there are cracks in my veins
a serious crack in my story but i ain't naming names.

doncha step on the cracks ya break your mama's back
doncha step on the cracks.
ain't no surprises in my cracker jacks.
polly wants a cracker
but polly's cracked.

well there are cracks in the loopholes you can crawl in between
and there are cracks in the fabrics of the girl of my dreams.

there are cracks in the memories of all the places i've slept.
so i hide between the sheets of all the secrets i've kept.

well there are cracks in my voice
lotsa cracks in my past.
so i'm hanging my head inside the crack of my ass.
at the crack of a bat ya just take off and fly
'til ya just disappear through that crack in the sky.

doncha step on the cracks ya break your mama's back
don't step on 'em
ain't no surprises in my cracker jacks.
polly wants a cracker and i'm just cracked...

Cuz Rock is Dead

the camera man is on a roll
but this ain't rock it's video.
ain't nothin' happenin' in rock and roll
stay home make a casserole.

we're here to sweat
if you ain't ready
just stay home homes
and make spaghetti.

cuz rock is dead
rock is dead.
hey elvis get off the bathroom floor and help us. cuz rock is dead.

my ears are shot
my soup is hot.
what's that you're playin' it sure ain't rock.

the voice of reason
a troubadour
say whatsa matter, man?
this rock don't roll.

cuz rock is dead
yeah rock is dead. you've turned into your parents
you're all lima beans and carrots. and rock is dead.

rock's on the ropes
it just ain't well. still got the swagger and you sound like hell!
can't feel no pulse
your heart's been bled
ain't nobody told ya that rock is dead?

ya beat your head against the wall
cinderella missed another ball.
tore down the rock club
built a shopping mall.
cuz rock is dead

yeah rock is dead
you've turned into your parents.
elvis get off the bathroom floor and help us.
cuz rock is dead...

Daddy Only Dreamin'

mommy flashin' red lights daddy wavin' white flags
do ya smell trouble? no i only smell a rat.
pink tights hot flesh burnin' from the wicked stench
mommy flashin' flash flesh
daddy burnin' bridges.

so now ya got a private audience
she already in the past tense.
she so catholic she so tense you ain't hard and she ain't wet.

a stand-in dummy gonna take your place
another song and dance to face.
do i sound bitter do i sound harsh?
just another stuffed shirt with too much starch.

another lousy bleedin' heart
get out quick if you're so smart.
i see ya shudder did i touch a nerve?
i'm straight up baybee i just missed a curve.
do i sound bitter do i sound bold?
bruised and battered and beaten and old?

do i seem shattered do i seem cold?
like a brand new scene from the same old show.
a beach bum basking in the snow
i'll pay the piper with playtime dough. melt her down until she froze

i'll pay my money and not pass go. mommy runnin' red lights
daddy burnin' bridges.

daddy only dreamin' 'bout how he's gonna burn you down.
don't kick that sleepin' dog
he only wants to burn you down. daddy only dreamin.'

Empty Handed Again

i can't stop this high-speed head-on crash.
dreams get dashed when you're too slow to react.
i got the will but i ain't got the ticket
i should give you my life but i only gotta minute.

i'm empty handed again.

i crack like glass ya always get the best of me.
i shine like ice in my sea of misery.
got my hands jammed deep down in my pockets
i ain't got no dough to buy you chocolates.

i'm empty handed again.

and even the tinman's heart is beating
the whole globe screams for the dreams we're seeking.
the sounds of silence can you feel your heart
STOP.
the weary world weeps for the love we lost.

i don't think i can lose my deceit
my head ya know it's harder than old concrete.
and baybee i could write you a sexxxy love letter
i wouldn't mean a word but i'll feel better.

when the sun don't shine you know my heart goes black
like a lion tamer looking for a whip to crack.

i'm empty handed again
i swear it's a sin
i'm empty handed again...

For My Beloved Son, Sean Robert

i failed as your daddy
and i failed as her boyfriend, too.
i failed at jumping through hoops
but i'm not gonna fail with you, Sean
no i'm not gonna fail with you.

not this time around.

i failed as a man sometimes
got pretty goddamn good at telling lies.
yeah i failed at telling the truth
but i'm not gonna fail with you.

again!

i failed to see all your angles
beat myself black and blue.
i failed at not giving up
but i'm not gonna fail with you.

i learned my lessons well.

i failed as a saint baybee
failed my life from her point of view
i'm trying hard to hold my head high
cuz i don't wanna fail with you.

not this time.

dead flowers and coffee for one
she is gone.
empty bed
i nailed her to the cross
now i'm lost.

i'm not gonna fail with you...

For Sheilia

you're the paper and i'm the eraser
here comes sheilia and i can't face her.

an iron in the fire a hat in the ring.
one horse in the race
one more white girl i can't face.

my ring on her finger and chains on my feet.
out of her life without missing a beat.

baby sure cured me sure cured me of that
i bet i can sink even lower than that.

you're the paper and i'm the eraser
here comes sheilia and of course i can't face her.
i'm gonna have to rub you out
i betcha i can't rub you out
i wish that i could rub her out.

you're the blank paper
and i'm the eraser...

A Hole to Crawl In

i'm just lookin' for a hole to crawl in.
i'll settle for some drums that i can rock on.
gimme one lousy street that i can walk on.
i need just one song in my heart.
one look one touch
hey honey what's so hard?

yeah i'm lookin' for a hole to crawl in.
deep down under where it's warm and safe.
i'm just lookin'
i'm just lookin'
i'm just lookin' for a hole' that i can crawl in.

i own it i dug it who needs it? who wants it?
not little old me.

now i'm lookin' for a hole that i can thrive in.
i'll settle for a friend that ain't a pigeon.
one fact of life that won't betray me.
i'll try to hold out for just a little bit more.

i'm still lookin' for a hole that i can thrive in
hop in a hot rod to hell and just drive in.
ya say you're lookin' for a hole that you can crawl in too?
i'll meetcha down under where it's warm and safe.

i'm just lookin' i'm just lookin' i'm just lookin' around
for your hole to crawl in.
i own it i dug it who needs it? who wants it?
not me.

i'm lookin' for any old hole to crawl in
to swallow me whole...

i'm just lookin' for any kinda hole to crawl in.

I Love Myself

i'm a liar and i'm a thief
a little bitch a brutal beast
when i play prince i need to rule
i gather subjects and then i treat 'em cruel. i love myself
i really love myself
if i don't do it nobody will
so i love myself
every goddamn day.

well i'm a lizard and i'm a snake
i never give i only take
call me chameleon
but i can't change
i'd kill myself but i'm too vain.

i love myself
i really love myself
if i don't do it who the hell will?
so i love myself
all the time.

well i'm a jerk
a peeping tom
5 4 3 2 1
a ticking time bomb
oh how i love myself

i ain't the christ child
but i might be god
and loving me's a fucking full-time job. i love myself
oh how i love myself
if you can't do it i still will
i love myself
no reason no rhyme...
i love myself

I'm A.J. Foyt

well i'm the gas down hero of my neighborhood.
ya best back down zero cuz i'm faster than you.
i'm bigger badder meaner and i'm smarter, too.

I'm aj foyt
i'm a man not a boy.
doncha send a boy to do a man's job.
i'm bigger than the beatles and i'm smarter than god.

i got arms like sequoia trees got shoulders to match
i'm a gizzly bear fighter pilot
and i live to go fast.

i'm aj foyt
i'm still a man not a boy
doncha send a boy to do a man's job.
i'm bigger than the beatles and i'm smarter than god.

i'm a texan a legend
i'm all guts balls and flash
i'm the only living racer
who still stands on the gas.

turn one i'm goin' out to the wall
i'm gonna send you to the hospital.
i'm the reigning king of speed
a dying breed.
i'm the only hero that america needs.
i'm a.j. foyt...

John Lennon

when you were 21 with your coke and rum playing "walk don't run" so
rockin'
then you were 22 in your mohair suit "from me to you" so pretty...
still only 22 in your beatles boots singin' "she loves you" so perfect...

johnny johnny when ya coming back? we all need a hero who won't turn his
back
johnny johnny woncha please come back?
johnny woncha please come home
johnny woncha please johnny woncha please johnny woncha please come
home?

when you were 23 the world was at your feet invented mersey beat the world
was at your feet so edgy.
still only 23 not only Beatles bleed singin' "please please me," so poppy.
they shot the wrong mop top it's paul they shoulda shot
straight to the top of the pops so deadly...

johnny johnny can't ya hear me call? cuz now ya got nothin' but once you
had it all
you wore your crown so gracefully we found out even jesus bleeds...
johnny johnny when ya coming back?
we need a hero who won't turn his back.
johnny johnny woncha please come back?
johnny woncha please johnny woncha please johnny woncha please come
home?

Life Imitates Art

well she's plaster of paris
oh no she's clay in my hands
she's oil and water when she slips through my hands.

well she's the mona lisa
she's venus de milo with arms
she's like a dime store statue with a zero dollar heart
dollar heart (gotta zero dollar heart).

she's classic post-modern that's why she's breaking my heart
i'll scream 'til i'm blue life imitates art
life imitates art.

thought i could mold you bend shape and fold you
it's the same old story i'm glad you slipped through my hands (oh baybee)
she's like some cheap andy warhol gotta killer cold blooded heart
hell she laughs when i fall apart
i'll squeal to the world life imitates art

life imitates art
she's hard as acrylic that's why she's breaking my heart.

life imitates art. life imitates art...
like truman capote

Life on the Rocks

hey buddy hey pal how 'bout another shot?
who's that is that me?
another life on the rocks.

i'm a gin rum dummy i'm a bloody mary whore
who's counting? not me
i'g getting stiff as a board.

another life on the rocks
another life on the rocks
another life.

slam 'em hard slam 'em fast
gimme three more drinks
i'm like a drowning man on a sinking ship.

i got sin coursing through my veins
mr. slick mister big that's me
hey baby what's your name?

my glass is empty i can feel rock bottom doncha
cry the blues to me, man i already got 'em.

i ain't hungry i just want more gin
life kills woe is me break out the violins.
got a sad, mad story your heart's gonna bleed
oh no that's my life story gushing out of me.

my glass is empty i can see rock bottom
doncha cry the blues to me, man i already got 'em another life
on the rocks...
another life on the rocks
another life...

Rob McCuen

Money Can't Buy Me

look who's on the loose again
hanging from a noose again.
dancing in the mean streets
searching out the creeps and freaks.

tryin' to forget who we are
tryin' to forget who we are.

prop me up and plug me in
a cardboard cutout of a man again.
cutting corners and swinging deals
chasing every dream on wheels.
down the road to nowhere. down the road to nowhere. fashion
plates and hip-hop kids
drunken jocks and loud mouth chicks.
love for sale at twenty buck a trick
boy oh boy another night on the town
boy oh boy another night on the town.

the smarter i get the more i drink.

Look who's in the dark again
circling like a mud shark again.
a hit of this a shot of that
a bloody nose and needle tracks.

trying to forget who i've lost
look who's dressed to kill tonight
every cheap thrill that money can't buy...

The Monkey Sees

The monkey see and the monkey don't
he says he will but i betcha he won't.
the monkey shimmers and the monkey shines
he came of age back in '69.

the monkey crumbles and the monkey cracks
so strap that monkey to your back.
the monkey shivers and the monkey shakes
roll the monkey 'round in shake and bake.

the monkey rattles and the monkey rolls
that monkey needs to be cajoled.
the monkey throws tantrums and the monkey rocks
best keep that monkey in a box.
busy little monkey.

the monkey quivers and the monkey quakes
best put that monkey at the stake.
the monkey slithers and the monkey crawls
we got his number off the bathroom wall.

the monkey babbles and the monkey begs
his monkey business is all the rage.
best kill that little monkey before he comes of age. the monkey
thrills and the monkey thrives
ya off that fucking monkey but then still won't die. the monkey
rattles and the monkey rolls...

(O Boy) Are You a Man or a Mouse

you made the bed but that don't mean i wanna sleep in it
you wrote the book but that don't mean i wanna read it.

you say let's play house
i say break out the wrecking ball.
ain't no stopping me now, i'd rather burn it down.

o boy are you a man or a mouse? i told you before doncha make me say it
again.

had ya in my sights
think it's time to shoot ya down (yeah shoot me down).

bang bang you win
i shoulda known you'd shoot me down (shoot me down).

you say love is good
not me i'd rather sell it cheap (i'll sell it cheap).

i love this side of you now
watch me turn the other cheek (the other cheek).

o boy are you a man or a mouse? i told you before don't make me say it
again.
o boy are you a man or a mouse?

The Poison Pen

oh no here i go again
gonna spit some venom with my poison pen
my pen is my switchblade only weapon i got
she loves me she loves me she loves me not.

oh no here i go again
the green-eyed monster is alive again
my pen is my jackknife only weapon i got
she loves me she loves me she loves me not.

if my pen were a knife i could change your life
if my pen were a rope i could hang on to hope
but face it buddy boy, it's only a pen
and my pen ain't good for much of anything.

oh no here i go again
another day another year
i'm lookin' for something but i don't know what
ain't never gonna find it here.

my fear is my weapon only weapon i got
she loves me she loves me she loves me not.

oh no everywhere i go i get haunted by your eyes
they flash like neon deep sea green
drill right through me for a laser beam

everyplace i go i can't help but see 'em
they're so penetrating they should put 'em in a museum
i'm dead in your eyes but you're all i got
she loves me she loves me she loves me not...

Torch Song

i'm carrying a torch for you
still carrying a torch for you
what's a war torn soldier boy gonna do? just spend his whole life tryin' to get
over you.

i'm carrying the world on my back
still carrying the world on my back
whatever happened to the wind at my back?
i function better with a gun at my back...

so i say
come back pretty baby
cuz i'm a sucker for you
i'm such a sucker for you.

i'm carrying the weight of the world
i'm in love with a saint of a girl.
i'd walk on water for ya but ya know i can't swim
c'mon pretty angel baby let me back in.

i'm carrying a torch for you for you
still carrying a torch for you. what's a war torn martyr boy gonna do?
can't spend my whole life pining for you

so i say
c'mon back my little angel
i'm a sucker just to touch her. i'm a sucker for you.

When I'm Depressed

in a world of suction i get sucked right in
it's so easy to blow it when ya get sucked in
in a world of friction i get rubbed the wrong way
that's why i always blow up when i don't get my way.
in a world of friction.

columbus was wrong the world ain't round
it's a world full of squares designed to bring me down
it's a cartoon world my world is my own my teeth are the whitest how come
i'm alone?

you ain't gotta foggy notion why you're so depressed
you're the last one to know it when your life is a mess
ya been banished forever from the tinfoil people go
black-balled from a world ya want nothin' from (i don't want nothin' from it
put it right here)

in a world divided it's always me against them
just when ya get the door open the fucker just gets slammed
no i never get invited to where the shiny people go
feelin' so strip naked in my second-hand clothes

when i'm depressed
everything fades to black
everything pisses me off
everything moves too fast
i get possessed
i get obsessed when i'm depressed when i'm depressed...

White Trash

white trash
i wanna wallow in your crust.
white trash
baby can i join your club?

white trash
hell yeah a life of petty crime.
white trash
i dig your grease and grime.

white trash
don't try to tell me what to do.
white trash
y'all live on white trash stew.

white trash
ya'll know ignorance is bliss.
white trash
gotta nice white ass that you can kiss.

white trash
know how to get what they need.
white trash
ya stab 'em but they still won't bleed.

white trash
we beat our old ladies 'til they're purple.
white trash
they breed like gerbils.

hey baxter, when did you get outta prison?
i heard ya got a new job workin' on the tilt-a-whirl.
junior sho' nuff did run good at talladega on sunday...

The World is Full of Clowns

you're losing your charm you're losing your charm
you're losing your essence baybee and it's breaking my heart

you're losing your grace you're losing your grace
crawl into some new skin in case i fall from grace.

the world is full of clowns
and baybee i'm just one if the world is full of clowns
where the hell is my fun?

everybody's laughing everybody's laughing everybody's laughing but the joke's on you.

so you're saving your face for a rainy day
crawl into my new skin since i've fallen from grace
you're losing your grace you're losing my charm
fall into some new world where it's breaking my heart.

the world is full of clowns i'll just take what i can get
if the world is full of clowns
ya know i work without a net
the world is full of clowns....

About the Author

Rob McCuen was born in Mount Pleasant Iowa, the first born to Alice and Chuck McCuen. Alice was a beautiful, creative, and loving mother, and Chuck a successful, savvy business executive and a proud father. Rob's birth was a huge event in that he was the first grandchild and nephew on my sister Alice's side of the family.

Early on it was evident that our newest member of the family was both bright and precocious. After overhearing Rob converse with his mother at an early age, the neighbor next door remarked that he might become the President of the United States.

My first Christmas present to Rob was a wooden bench with colorful pegs that he could hammer on with a wooden mallet. I considered this to be an appropriate educational toy. Rob obviously found it not to be exciting enough. He found nailing the living room curtains to the wall with his new wooden mallet more entertaining.

Looking back, perhaps that was the beginning of his fascination with beating the drums. What we did know was that he was a handful.

Rob knew at the age of four that he wanted to be a drummer. His inspiration came from growing up listening to the Beatles, The Kinks, and The Who.

When he was nine, he learned that he was not eligible to play drums in the school band as they required two years of piano lessons as a prerequisite. Rob was not going to give up. His doting parents allowed him to take private lessons.

At eleven, he formed his own band. This group practiced every Saturday morning in the McCuens' basement. I was only there once early on to witness the practice and came to the conclusion his parents were saints for enduring this phase of Rob's life. He named that band the Fabulous Riverias. They made their debut at the Spring Sing at Mount Pleasant High School in Rob's senior year. Rob informed me they were a sensational hit.

After graduating in 1979 from Truman State University in Missouri, Rob moved to Champaign, Illinois, While there he drove a cab, did some networking, and worked at launching a career. In the fall of 1979, Rob moved to Milwaukee to audition for a band named the Shivvers. When that didn't work out, he began drumming and writing songs for the RPMs. The RPMs published a single that was purchased all over the world.

In 1982 Rob joined the renowned psychedelic pop group, Plasticland. Plasticland toured and sold records all over the globe. They were the critics' darlings. Rob tells me he was the token teen idol of the group. He continued to perform in various beat pop groups and is about to release his first solo record. In addition to this, he has been involved in 23 other releases.

Rob struggled most of his life with manic episodes, depression, anxiety, and broken relationships. He passed away in August 2021.

— Aunt Betty

www.ingramcontent.com/pod-product-compliance
Lightning Source LLC
Chambersburg PA
CBHW021337140626
46545CB00019B/1196